QUACKING UP!

Wacky Jokes
for Feathered Folks

First published 2002 by Walker Books Ltd
87 Vauxhall Walk, London SE11 5HJ
2 4 6 8 10 9 7 5 3 1
Jokes compiled by Rick Walton
Additional material by Charlie Gardner
© 2002 Universal Pictures Visual Programming Ltd
™ Sitting Ducks Productions
Licensed by Universal Studios Licensing LLLP
Printed and bound in Great Britain by Ebenezer Baylis Ltd
British Library Cataloguing in Publication Data:
a catalogue record for this book is available
from the British Library
ISBN 0-7445-8947-9

Contents

Foreword

Ed: Oly, why were you walking backwards? No wonder you fell over us!

Oly: I thought it would be real funny to walk backwards … in the Forward…

Ed: It's not a "Forward", it's a "Foreword" … you know, like an Intro-*duck*-tion.

Oly: Kewl! What are we doing that for?

Ed: Because Bill asked us to fill in.

Waddle: Filling? Make mine Pondroach Paté with Dragonfly Mayo on wholemeal!

Ed: You featherbrain! Why have you got that ruler with you?

Oly: He took it to bed … he wanted to see how long he slept.

Waddle: Yeah … and I took a pencil, too … to draw the curtains.

Ed: Aaagh! I think it's time to go.

Oly: But we haven't been intro*ducked*...

Waddle: Ma-llards, Ladies and Jellybeans...

Ed: ...we really hope this book quacks you up!

Oly: The ... End.

Ed: No it's not, it's the beginning, you dodo!

Waddle: Um, where's the "Backword"?

Ed: Turn the page, turn the page!

Quacking Up

What time does Bill get up?
At the quack of dawn.

What does Jerry hear
that sends him back to his cage?
The Door-Bill.

What should Bill do if Jerry hurts himself?
Re-parrot.

If Bill fell apart, what would you use
to put him back together?
Duck tape.

What pushes Bill out of bed in
the morning?
A billdozer.

Who would Bill become if he was
bitten by a vampire?
Count Quackula.

Where does Bill go
when he gets sick?
To a ducktor.

Which of Bill's friends is extinct?
Al-dodo.

What did Waddle say to Oly
after they'd eaten poison-ivy?
"You scratch my beak and I'll
scratch yours."

What would you get if you crossed
Waddle with an owl?
A wise-quack.

When Ed listens to music,
what does he use?
Ed-phones.

What's the difference
between a penniless duck
and Waddle's feathers?
One is hard up and the
other is soft down.

**Where did Oly learn
everything he knows?**
At Oly-mentary school.

Why does Ed want to be cloned?
Because two Eds are better than one.

Who likes to draw
pictures of milkshakes?
The Oly-strator.

If you're ever in trouble, why should
you call Oly?
So you'll have an Oly-bi.

How does Oly get to the top floor
of a building?
He takes the Oly-vator.

Why does Waddle get on his knees?
So he can eat his shortcake.

Why did Waddle feel sick?
Because his flies were bigger
than his stomach.

Why does Waddle
twirl around before
ordering deep-fried worm?
Because he knows that the whirly
bird gets the worm.

**How many milkshakes should Waddle
get for a pound?**
None. Pounds don't drink milkshakes.

**What happened when Waddle ate too
much sweetcorn?**
He got cob-webbed feet.

How does Waddle sneeze?
"I chew! I chew!"

Down
the Decoy

Why did Oly take
a ruler to the Decoy Café?
Because he wanted a square meal.

**What is black and white,
yellow and white, and green?**
Fred and Bill eating a pickle.

**What did Waddle do when he swallowed
his fork?**
He ate with his spoon.

Where does Bev do her baking?
In her breadroom.

**What has eight legs and goes crunch,
crunch, crunch, crunch?**
Bill, Ed, Oly and Waddle
eating crisps.

What's crunchy and delicious and goes, "Snap, Crackle and Hop?"
Frog Krispies.

Did you hear the joke about the deep-fried worm?
Never mind, you wouldn't swallow it.

What do ducks eat
when they want a hot meal?
Fireflies.

What's black and white and red
all over?
Fred eating a tomato.

How can you tell how many milkshakes
the ducks have ordered?
Look at the counter.

What do ducks like to put on
their toast?
Butterflies.

Why do ducks like to eat frogs?
Because it makes them hoppy.

Ducktown Races

What's white and yellow and carries Aldo around Ducktown?
An Automo-Bill.

What do alligators call ducks on scooters?
Meals-on-wheels.

What has six legs, two heads, and roars?
Bill and Aldo on a scooter.

What's black and white and has eight wheels?
Fred on roller-blades.

If Bill rides a scooter, what does Fred ride?
An Ice-cycle.

**Did you hear the joke
about the broken-down scooter?**
Never mind, it doesn't go anywhere.

**What's black and white
and red all over?**
Raoul sitting on a stop sign.

What kind of car does a duck drive?
A Pond-tiac.

**How do you make a Pond-tiac
speed up?**
Step on the quack-celerator.

**Did you hear the joke about the fastest
scooter in the world?**
Never mind, you wouldn't be
able to follow it.

Gator Gags

What do alligators like
to eat with their soup?
Quackers.

**What do you get if you
cross an alligator with an elephant?**
An animal that will remember
every duck he's ever eaten.

**What's long, green and scaly and
flies through the night sky?**
An owl-igator.

**What do you get if you cross an
alligator with a praying mantis?**
An animal that says grace
before he eats a duck.

**What do young alligators eat
at breaktime?**
Milk and quackers.

What's green,
scaly and very slippery?
An oily-gator.

What's long, green and scaly and
always coughing?
An ill-igator.

Why did the alligator eat the acrobat?
Because he wanted a well-balanced meal.

Who looks for criminals in Swamptown?
The Investi-gator.

Who does the Investi-gator turn
criminals over to?
The Interro-gator.

Who does the
Interro-gator hire if all else fails?
The Termi-gator.

What's the difference between
an alligator and an elevator?
Well, if you don't know,
you should probably
just take the stairs.

What's an alligator's
favourite kind of tree?
The evergreen.

What do young alligators like
to hear their cereal say?
Snap, Quackle and Pop.

Did you hear the joke
about the mean, angry alligator?
Never mind, it's not nice.

How do you find your way
around Swamptown?
Hire a Navi-gator.

Why don't alligators eat penguins?
Because they can't get the wrappers off.

What's the difference between
a millionaire and an alligator?
The millionaire has quite a bit,
while the alligator has
quite a bite.

**What do you get if you
cross a kangaroo with an alligator?**
Leaping lizards.

**Where can alligators sell their
used ducks?**
At a pond-broker's.

Why are alligators afraid of rabbits?
Because rabbits like to eat green things.

Do gators like to feed the ducks?
Yes ... to each other.

Why can't a gator use a mobile phone?
Because only a croc can dial.

Duck Tales All

What do you get when
you cross a buffalo with a duck?
A buffalo bill.

What happens if you drop a duck egg?
It quacks.

Why shouldn't you be afraid of ducks?
Because they're 'armless.

How do you learn about ducks?
Watch a duck-umentary.

How do you make a duck quack?
Drop him on concrete.

Why doesn't the backside of a duck look right?
Because it's upside down.

Why do ducks look grumpy?
Because they're always in fowl moods.

What do old ducks get if they race their scooters too much?
Vroom-atism.

What kind of doctor treats ducks?
A quack.

What would happen if a duck ate gunpowder?
She'd lay hand gren-eggs.

What would happen if you dropped the hand gren-eggs?
They would egg-splode.

What would happen if a
duck bit into a stick of dynamite?
It would be a-bomb-in-a-bill!

Why are duck feathers so cheap?
Because all you need is the
down payment.

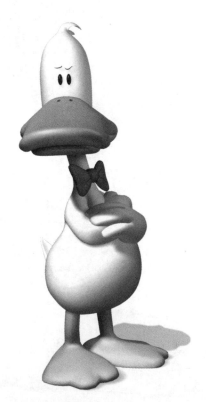

**Why should you call the
police if you see a duck with a toy?**
Because that's fowl play.

Why do ducks have webbed feet?
So they can use the Internet.

Why don't ducks play football?
Because they're not much good on
the wing.

Why do ducks have bills?
Because they keep buying things on credit.

What do fast ducks say?
"Quick quick!"

When is a duck not a duck?
When it's a chicken.

Did you hear about the tiger that ate a plateful of duck?
He was a duck-filled fatty-puss.

How do you make a duck sink?
Put it in your kitchen and attach it to a drainpipe.

Fun with Fred

What's Fred's favourite month?
Snow-vember.

What likes to write, and lives at the south pole?
A ballpoint penguin.

What's black and white
and makes you groan?
A pun-guin.

Why is a penguin careful not to get
into trouble?
Because he doesn't want to be in
hot water.

What did Bill sing at Fred's
birthday party?
"Freeze a jolly good fellow!"

Did you hear the joke about
Fred's apartment?
Never mind, it would only leave
you cold.

What did Bill say the first time he visited Fred's apartment?
"What an ice place you have!"

What does Fred listen to in his apartment?
Chill-out music.

Knock knock.
Who's there?
Fred.
Fred who?
Freddy or not, here I come!

**Did you hear the joke about
Fred's newspaper?**
Never mind, it's tear-able.

What's black and white and very sharp?
A pin-guin.

**Why did Bill take the letter "N" into
Fred's apartment?**
Because it made the ice Nice.

What's black and white and
dirty all over?
A pig-pen-guin.

Where do pig-pen-guins live?
At the sows pole.

And what do pig-pen-guins live in?
Pig-loos.

What's black and white and red all over?
Fred with the measles.

What's black and white and black and
white and black and white and black
and white and black and blue?
Fred falling downstairs.

What's black, then white,
then yellow, then black, then
white, then yellow...
Fred rolling downhill
with a daisy in his mouth.

Pond Puns

Why do ducks swim on the water?
Because it's too hard to walk on it.

What's one of the nicest things you can say to a duck?
Go jump in a lake.

What's small, gold-coloured, and swims in ponds?
A baby alligator wearing lots of jewellery.

Would a duck swim on a full stomach?
No, it would swim on water.

Did you hear the joke about the duck pond?
Never mind, it's too deep for you.

Bill
and Aldo

How did Bill make Aldo cross?
He showed him where the bridge
was and kicked him in the tail.

How did Aldo get brainy?
He ate a school of fish.

Why does Aldo protect Bill?
Because he's his buddy-guard.

Who takes care of Aldo when he's sick?
Florence Nighten-gator.

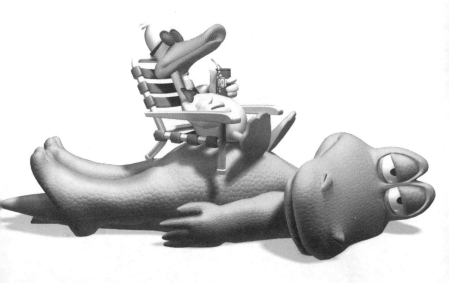

Why doesn't Aldo eat Bill?
Because it would give him a billy-ache.

Why did Aldo hire a secretary?
Because he needed someone to file
his teeth.

**Why does Bill stay away from
Aldo's mouth?**
Because of All-do's teeth.

Why is Aldo a good storyteller?
Because he has quite a tail.

**What does Bill have as much of as
an alligator?**
The letter "l".

What is the difference between a rainy day and Aldo with toothache?
One pours with rain and the other roars with pain.

Ducks
and Gators

If a duck visited an alligator
around noon, what would he be?
Lunch.

**How did the alligator
feel after he ate the duck?**
Down in the mouth.

**Why didn't the alligator eat the
millionaire duck?**
Because he was dieting and wanted to
stay away from rich foods.

**What do you get if you cross an
alligator with a duck?**
One less duck.

**Why won't alligators eat ducks
they've argued with?**
Because they don't like food that
disagrees with them.

**What did the alligator
say to the duck?**
"Pleased to eat you."

**What did the duck say when the
alligator bit him on the tail?**
"That's the end of me!"

What happened to
the duck who kicked the
alligator in the mouth?
He was de-feeted.

Why did the gator lie next to the duck?
He wanted to have a bite before going
to sleep.

Why did the alligator try to eat Bill?
Because he wanted to win the No-Bill prize.

**How can a duck get a set of teeth
put in?**
By teasing an alligator. The alligator will
then put his teeth into the duck.

What's white, hides in trees and pounces on passing alligators?
A sabre-tooth duck.

What's puffed up and full of feathers and lies on a bed?
An alligator who's sick from eating too many ducks.

Where does a 50-stone duck sit?
Anywhere it wants.

What's black and scaly with big flippers?
An alligator in a wet suit.

Howl
with Raoul

**What would you get if
Raoul and an owl got together?**
Two birds in caw-hoots.

**What makes Raoul
stick with his friends?**
Vel-crow.

What makes a crow different from a duck?
The crow-mosomes.

What kind of music do crows listen to?
Rock 'n' Raoul.

**What do you get if you plant an angry
crow in your garden?**
Crow-cusses.

Where's Raoul from?
Mexi-crow.

What's Raoul's favourite game?
Crow-quet.

Who arrests crows in the corn field?
The corn cop.

Who brings Christmas presents to Raoul?
Santa Caws.

Why is Raoul like a coin when he's sitting on a fence?
Because he has a head on one side and a tail on the other.

What do you get if you cut a crow in half?
Ow!

**Did you hear the joke
about the flock of flying crows?**
Never mind, it would go right
over your head.

Feathered and Famous

Who was the bird that helped Robin Hood?
Friar Duck.

Who is covered with feathers, lays eggs and helps pull Father Christmas's sleigh on Christmas Eve?
Rudolph the Red-nosed Rein-duck.

Who's Bill's favourite author?
Charles Duckens.

What did Charles Duckens write?
Great Egg-spectations.

Who was the greatest duck explorer?
Sir Francis Drake.

What's huge and white,
lives in the ocean and flies
south for the winter?
Moby Duck.

Who rules in the land of ducks?
The Duck-tator.

Later Gator

How can you tell if an alligator is following you?
Listen for the quacks. If there are no quacks, it's not a duck ... so it must be an alligator.

What's long, looks like a lizard, has big teeth and lives in a swamp?
A dinosaur.

Did you hear the joke about the alligator's broken tooth?
Never mind, you wouldn't see the point.

Who do the alligators call when Swamptown is overrun with cockroaches?
The Fumi-gator.

Ali Gator	If you buy my duck's bill I'll throw in the rest of the duck.
Al E. Gator	How much do you want for the duck's bill?
Ali Gator	**Ten dollars.**
Al E. Gator	Ten dollars! That's too much!
Ali Gator	**No it's not, it's a ten-dollar bill.**